# The Peloponnese

**Alice Whitman**

# THE PELOPONNESE

**KEDROS**

**Edited & Designed by** *N. Eliopoulos — B. Kagia*
**Photography by** *A. Spyropoulos — G. Sfikas — Ph. Letzis — M. House*
**Cover by** *D. Kalokyris*
**4-Colour Maps, Illustrations and Typeset by** *Photokyttaro LTD*
*219 Hymettus st., Athens 11632*

**Printed by** *A. & P. Spyrou*

**Published by Cedar Books**
A division of Kedros Publishers Inc.
3 Gennadiou St.
Athens, 10678


**Distributed by**
**Kedros Publishers Inc.**
3 Gennadiou st., Athens 10678
Tel. 36.09.712, 36.02.007 — FAX 36.31.981

# Contents

Kephallonia
Patraïkos Kolpos
Antirio
Rio
Patra
Kato Salmenikos
Aiyo
Diakophto
Daphnes
Kalogria
Kato Akhaïa
Pteri
Leontio
Selinus
Vuraïkos
Lapas
Halandritsa
Kalanistra
Mega Spilaio
Kalavryta
Koloussio
Moni Ag. Lavras
Santamerio
Kartezi
Kyllene
Lehena
Pinios
Kalentzi
Lagovouni
Zakynthos
Andravida
Loutra Kyllenes
Gastouni
Lykouria
Amaliada
Daphne
Kourouta
Erimanthos
Kantila
Ladonas
Katakolo
Pyrgos
Alphios
Olympia
Langadia
Vytina
Makrisia
Krestena
Dimitsana
Anditsena
Kato Samiko
Kaïafa
Davia
Karitena
Kakovatos
IONIO PELAGOS
Lepreo
Nedas
Megalopoli
Lykosoura
Assea
Kyparissiakos Kolpos
Issari
Vlachokerasi
Psari
Kalo Nero
Kyparisia
Meligalas
Dyrachio
Mavromati
Philiatra
Kastorio
Androusa
Pamisos
Artemisia
Gargaliani
Messini
Kalamata
Mistras
Vlachopoulo
Rizomelos
Mantinia
Petalidi
Kampos
Pylos
Kardamyli
Ag. Pelagia
Potamos
Diakophti
Ag. Nikolaos
Methoni
Koroni
Phinikous
Kastania
Vassilitsio
Kythera
Kapsali
Trakhila
Messeniakos Kolpos
Limeni
Areopoli
Pyrgos Dyrou
Dryalos
Mezapos
Antikythera
Gerolymenas
Galaniana

rinthiakos Kolpos
Xilokastro
Rethio
Kiato
Vouliagmeni
Perakhora
Loutraki
Megara
Pireaus
Salamina
Soulio
Asopos
Korinthos
Kaliani
Solomos
Galatas
Nemea
Sophiko
Dervenakia
Limnes
Aegina
Nea Epidauros
Palaea Epidauros
Argos
Lygourio
Tyrins
Nauplio
Tolo
Poros
Kalloni
Mili
Akhladokampos
Galatas
Kato Doliana
Astros
Astros Beach
Korakovouni
Ag. Andreas
Kranidi
Ermioni
Porto Heli
Hydra
Tyros beach
Spetses
nvakou
Leonidi
Bassaras
Argolikos Kolpos
Poulithra
Ag. Anargyroi
Geraki
Kyparissi
Paralia
Eurotas
Krokees
Metamorphosi
Gytheio
Monemvasia
Ayeranos
Archagelos
Lakonikos Kolpos
Elafonessos
Velanidia
hia

# Peloponnese

Although the Peloponnese is connected to mainland Greece by the slender Isthmus of Corinth, its name (in Greek, *"Pelops' island"*, after the legendary hero Pelops) suggests that the Greeks have always regarded the Peloponnese to be separate from the mainland in just the way that an island is. Today, like an island, the Peloponnese remains something of a world unto itself, although thus far it has not suffered the touristic invasions that have brought new hotels, discos, frayed nerves, and fast food cafeterias to many a Greek island. It's hard to know why the Peloponnese remains just a bit underexplored, because it has everything one comes to Greece to find: sandy beaches, quiet harbours with fishing boats, seaside tavernas with retsina wine, mountain villages, and spectacular ancient sites. Excellent roads, a good public bus network, and hydrofoil service from Piraeus to *Leonidion*, *Kiparissia*, and *Monemvassia* on the east coast, and from Crete to *Gythion* on the south coast, make getting around the Peloponnese easy and pleasant. All but the most remote villages have comfortable hotels, and a string of seaside camping sites make it unnecessary (and illegal!) for visitors to search for places to pitch their tents.

There are as many ways to enjoy the Peloponnese as there are visitors to the Peloponnese. Some will want to head for the seaside, especially for the beaches near *Porto Kheli* in the *Argolid, Loutraki* in *Corinthia, Astros and Aghios Andreas* in *Arcadia,* and *Gythion* in *Laconia.* Others will head inland, to explore the mountain ranges of *Parnon* and *Taÿetos*, or underground to the *caves of Dirou* – always keeping in mind that no one should undertake such expeditions alone, or without the proper equipment. Those who find such activities too strenuous, may prefer to lounge about at one of the mineral spas, such as Loutraki, and take a real rest cure. And, almost all

*1. Nauplion: a spectacular sunset with Bourtzi in the background.*
2. Following pages: *a magnificent view of Nauplion Town with its modern hotels and a medieval fortress.*

who visit the Peloponnese will want to visit its important classical sites – and may discover to their surprise that there are a number of important monuments from later periods, such as the Byzantine site of *Mistras* and the *Frankish castles* of the *Morea*.

The climate of the Peloponnese is all that one dreams of about Greece: hot dry summers, warm, clear autumns, mild springs, and crisp winters. While it is true that, with bad luck, one might huddle miserably in the rain for days in the winter or early spring, it is equally true that one could sit outdoors in December and enjoy the winter sun. In addition, those who visit the Peloponnese off-season will be rewarded with uncrowded museums, sites, and beaches – and, in the spring, with Greek wildflowers growing in places that in summer are bare and brown. The summer winds, such as the *Meltemi*, and the *Livas*, can be hot and parching, and in some areas, such as the Mani, the winds are almost always fierce. Elsewhere, there are usually breezes, especially welcome in summer. In short, on a visit to the Peloponnese at any time of year, all one has to do is relax, and enjoy Pelops' island.

The Peloponnese is almost as wide as it is long, with a total territory of 8,278 square miles (21,500 sq. kms), much of it rugged mountain ranges running down to the sea. The Peloponnesian peninsula is the southernmost extension of the Balkans, and ends in three small peninsulas which extend into the sea like Poseidon's trident. The mountains of the Peloponnese form part of the Dinaric, or Hellenic Alpine range, with Taïyetos and Parnon running north-south, and the Argolic-Arcadian range running east-west. The ranges intersect and interlock, so that one range follows upon another as far as the eye can see; in some cases, as at Sparta, the mountain ranges almost seem to encircle the horizon. The mountains are largely limestone, with less marble than on the islands, or in Attica, and many of the Peloponnesian cliffs are a distinctive rusty red. There are more river beds than actual rivers in the Peloponnese today, although in antiquity Arcadia and Laconia

*3. Part of the Agora and shops in the NW part of ancient Corinth. The remaining columns of the archaic Temple of Apollo are in the background.*

*4. An awesome view from the "Rock" of Monemvassia.*

were famously well-watered. The east and south coasts of the Peloponnese are particularly rugged, with few decent harbours, whereas the north coast along the Gulf of Corinth has a coastal plain, and the west coast has the deep-water ports of Kalamata and Patras. The Peloponnese is bounded by the Aegean to the east, the broad Ionian to the west, the Sea of Crete to the South, and the Gulf of Corinth to the north, and each of these bodies of water is perfectly capable of turning from glassy calm to dangerous whitecaps in a matter of minutes.

A million of Greece's 9 million citizens live in the Peloponnese – a startlingly small number in comparison to the 3 million Greeks (many originally from the Peloponnese) who live in Athens. As a result, many once-flourishing villages in the mountains of Arcadia and Laconia, or along the shores of the Mani, are today virtually deserted except for a handful of old men and women. All that emigration to Athens and abroad (there are more Peloponnesian Greeks in Chicago than in the Peloponnese) stems from the lack of significant job opportunities for those not engaged in farming and fishing – and the growing reluctance of many young Greeks to pursue these traditional and unremunerative activities. It's as hard to make a decent living farming in most of the Peloponnese today as it was in the 8th century B.C. when the poet *Hesiod* wrote that "The gods have hidden the means of life from men." And as for fishing, years of over-fishing the coastal waters of the Peloponnese (including dynamiting for fish) has reduced the bounty of the sea to dangerous levels. The great French oceanographer Jacques Cousteau has warned that the Mediterannean is well on its way to becoming a dead sea by the year 2000.

The port town of Patras is the Peloponnese's largest city (and Greece's third largest), with some 112,000 inhabitants. In some ways, Patras is the Peloponnese's *only* real city, and Corinth, Sparta, Tripoli, Pyrgos, Kalamata, and Argos feel much more like overgrown towns than cities. It must be admitted that, with the exception of Nauplion and Sparta, the larger towns of the Peloponnese lack charm. Argos and Corinth, as well as many of the towns along the Gulf of Corinth, have been repeatedly levelled by earthquakes, and hastily rebuilt with little thought to beauty. It is the small towns, such as Gythion,

*5. An orange grove outside Sparta. Snow-capped Mt. Taïyetos is in the background.*

and villages, such as *Andritsaina*, that most visitors will find most charming – although after a long day touring, many will be pleased to stay in the new hotels in the larger towns.

The Peloponnese is divided into seven nomes, or districts, and each still has the basic boundaries it did in antiquity, although to complicate matters, a sliver of the Nome of Corinthia extends across the Peloponnese along the northern shore of the Gulf of Corinth – and the off-shore islands of Hydra, Poros, Spetses, and Kythera are administered by the Nome of Piraeus. Many first-time visitors will hardly be aware of these divisions, but each nome has its own character, and Arcadia is no more like the Argolid than Vermont is like Indiana, or Cornwall like Kent. The two eastern nomes (the *Argolid* and *Corinthia*) have gentle landscapes, with wheat fields and olive groves; *Achaia*, to the northwest, is less fertile, while its neighbor *Elis* has fertile farm land; *Messenia* to the southwest has rivers and plains, while *Laconia* to the extreme south, and central *Arcadia are* dominated by the severe ranges of *Taïyetos* and *Parnon*.

Most visitors will begin their visit to the Peloponnese by crossing the narrow Isthmus of Corinth, and then doing a circuit of the Peloponnese with expeditions inland to some of the major sites. And most visitors, as they wander through *Corinth* and *Argos, Mycenae* and *Mistras*, will find themselves wishing that they'd brushed up on some Greek history and mythology before their visit. Just how long have people lived in the Peloponnese? Did *Agamemnon* really live at Mycenae? Did the *Persian Wars* come before the *Peloponnesian War*, or was it the other way around? And what were the *Labors of Herakles*, and where did they take place? And why are there Frankish castles in the Peloponnese, of all places? Perhaps a few words on the history of the Peloponnese are in order.

6. *Flowers bloom all around the Byzantine ruins on the slopes of Mistras.*
7. Following Pages: *The partly restored Hellenistic Palaistra (wrestling grounds) in ancient Olympia.*

## A Little History

We know that people were living in the Peloponnese 25,000 years B.C. because of remains found in the Franchthi Cave in the Argolid. The spectacular caves of Dirou in the Mani have yielded Neolithic remains from the 4th millenium B.C., and an entire "palace" at Lerna, in the Argolid, has been found dating from the same period. What we do *not* know is what these people were like – although we know from the presence of the *Lerna* palace that they lived in settlements, and raised crops, as opposed to wandering the land in search of sustenance. But what these people thought, or worshipped, is lost to us, because we have no written records for them, and only insufficient archaeological remains. Still, we know from the Dirou cave that these early Greeks were painters (the cave walls are decorated) and sculptors (the remains of stone figurines have been found), and that they made tools of obsidian to use in hunting, fishing, and farming. And from the Lerna palace we have a terracotta statuette of a woman, probably a goddess, (now in the Argos museum) to give us a tantalizing glimpse of what these people thought their deities looked like so many thousands of years ago.

Excavated settlements from the Peloponnese's earliest period of occupation are few, and it is impossible to know how thickly or thinly settled the peninsula was. However, enough settlements have been excavated from the Early Bronze Age (2800-2000 B.C.) to suggest that by this period the Peloponnese had a great number of villages. And, in the following centuries, known as the Middle and Late Bronze Ages (c. 2000-1100 B.C.) the Peloponnese knew its first great period of power: the Mycenaean era. These were the years of the pre-eminence of Mycenae, home of King Agamemnon, and the greatness of *Nestor's Pylos*. These are the years, in short, remembered by *Homer's* epic poems, the *Iliad* and the *Odyssey*. The two poems tell the story of the ten-year Trojan War which began when Helen, the wife of Sparta's king Menelaus, fell in love with *Paris of Troy*, and ended with the death of the hero

*8. A Byzantine church inside the fort of Pylos.*

*9. The approach to the Lion Gate at the ancient site of Mycenae.*

*10. The Theatre of Epidauros: the best preserved of all Greek theatres dating from the 4th-century B.C.*

*Achilles*, Helen's return to Sparta, and Odysseus' delayed return to his wife *Penelope* and his home in *Ithaca*. Homer's epics tell how Agamemnon, King of Mycenae, led the great expedition to conquer Troy and reclaim Helen – and over the years excavations have yielded astonishing finds to substantiate much of what Homer had to say. For years archaeologists thought that Homer's description of a "boar's tooth helmet" was poetic license – until just such a helmet (now on view in the Nauplion museum) was found at the Mycenaean site of *Tiryns*. And for years scholars thought that Homer's description of Mycenae as "rich in gold" was hyperbolic – until the golden treasures of Mycenae (now on view in the National Archaeological Museum in Athens) were unearthed.

The Mycenaean era seems to have ended abruptly and violently about the end of the 12th century B.C., for reasons we still do not understand. Why were so many palaces – Mycenae and Pylos, for example – abandoned? Some seem to have been burnt – but by whom? With no written record to help us understand these events (for the Linear B tablets found at Mycenaean sites do not offer narrative, but provide only lists of goods stored in palace warehouses), we are at something of a loss to understand what clearly was a great disaster for the Mycenaean settlements. It is possible that the settlements fell before a wave of invaders, the people known as the Dorians, believed to have swept into Greece at about this period from Northern Europe, burning, pillaging, and conquering – and, ultimately, settling, intermarrying, and assimilating.

Greek mythology preserves a memory of the Dorian invasion in the legends of the Return of the Sons of Herakles. The story goes that Herakles had left the Peloponnese to pursue new adventures, and that generations later, his sons returned to claim their patrimony. It's an interesting myth, because at one and the same time it attempts to explain the invasions – and to put a good face on them, by suggesting that the invaders were *not* dreadful outlanders and barbarians, but returning Greeks. Certainly, as the process of assimilation went forward, the Dorians became Greek, and by the time, for exam-

*11. The lighthouse of Perachora, near the ancient site of Heraion.*

ple, of the relatively recent 8th century B.C., the Dorian dialect of Greek was the language of the Peloponnese.

Beginning in the 8th century, and continuing into the 7th, a number of powerful cities grew up in the Peloponnese, cities almost as powerful in their day as Mycenae had been in its. Some of the most powerful were Corinth, Sparta, and Argos, and these cities were sufficiently large that they began to feel the need for new territory. Often, instead of attacking neighbors, they established overseas colonies in southern Italy and Sicily – especially in areas which had fertile farmland and good harbours. This was the period of the great *tyrants* in Greece, strong leaders who introduced coinage, expanded trade, and began to ornament their cities with the great temples, public squares, and shrines whose remains draw so many tourists today.

By the beginning of the 5th century, one city had emerged as the most powerful in the Peloponnese: Sparta, overshadowing Corinth and Argos. The Persian Invasions (490 and 480 B.C.) never threatened the Peloponnese, thanks to the concerted Greek effort which halted the invaders at Marathon and Salamis. However, the lengthy *Peloponnesian War* (431-404 B.C.) between Athens and its allies and Sparta and its allies not only left Athens defeated, but Sparta exhausted. In the next century, much of the Peloponnese fell under the rule of one of the great military geniuses of antiquity: *Epaminondas* of *Thebes*. Bit by bit, Epaminondas conquered Sparta's former Peloponnesian holdings, and built a string of astonishing new cities at *Megalopolis*, *Messene*, and *Mantineia*; Epaminondas hoped to break old loyalties by settling people from all over the Peloponnese in his new cities, however, no one wanted to live in the new towns – and, after Epaminondas' death in battle in 462 B.C., almost no one did.

In a sense, Epaminondas was but one in a long series of invaders and conquerors – beginning with the Dorians, and ending with the Turks – to ravage the Peloponnese. After Epaminondas, the Peloponnese (along with all Greece) fell to *Phi-*

*12. The castle of Larissa, overlooking the city of Argos. The monastery of Panayia i Kekrimeni is on the right.*

13. A panoramic view of Mistras.

*lip of Macedon* and his son *Alexander the Great*, although both Philip and Alexander were more interested in expanding their empire outside Greece than in dominating the Peloponnese. Their empire, ruled and misruled by their successors, fell finally to the *Romans*, who conquered all Greece in 146 B.C. The Romans moved into Greece with their usual efficiency and zeal, putting up aqueducts, building roads, expanding towns, ornamenting temples, and putting up statues of emperors wherever possible. Greece, in short, was merely one among many Roman provinces. As throughout the Roman Empire, Christianity began to get a toe-hold in the Peloponnese, and the great traveller Saint Paul visited Corinth on several occasions. Many temples were converted to Christian churches, and impressive Christian basilicas were built in important centers such as Corinth, and even in remote areas such as the Mani.

As the Roman Empire expanded to take in almost all the known world from Britain to India, administration became increasingly difficult. Finally, the empire was divided for governmental efficiency, and administered from two capitals: the old capital of *Rome*, and the new capital of *Constantinople*. After the 4th century A.D., the Peloponnese, along with the rest of Greece, was administered from Constantinople, during the centuries of what was known as the *Byzantine Empire*. Within little more than another hundred years, the western empire headed by Rome had fallen to the barbarian *Goths*, and the eastern empire was all that remained. In the centuries that followed, all too often, Greece was neglected, and buffeted by repeated invasions: *Visigoths, Goths,* and *Slavs* invaded and, like the Dorians long before them, often settled and stayed.

After Constantinople fell in 1204 to rampaging Venetian, Genoese, and Frankish soldiers from the forces of the Third Crusade, the *Franks* and *Venetians* attempted the conquest of Greece, and began to occupy the Peloponnese. They established a profitable silk trade throughout the peninsula, planting groves of the mulberry trees, from whose name, *morea*, the Peloponnese itself took its name, the *Morea*, during these years. In addition, the Venetians coveted the rich harbours of the Peloponnese's western and southern shores for their maritime empire. Consequently, the next centuries saw almost continuous fighting, as the Franks and Venetians tried to hold the Peloponnese. The Franks particularly built massive castles to protect their holdings, and many remain to this day at Nauplion and Monemvassia, Methoni and Koroni, and on scattered hill-tops throughout the Peloponnese. Finally, in the 13th century, the great Byzantine emperor *Michael VII Palaeologus* drove the Franks out of the Peloponnese, and ruled from Mistras, where the last emperor of Byzantium, Constantine Palaeologus, was crowned a hundred years later. Constantine had the sad distinction of losing Constantinople to the Turks in 1453, and thereafter the Peloponnese, along with the entire empire, was ruled from Turkey.

During the long years of the Turkish occupation, only a few remote areas of the Peloponnese, notably the Mani, escaped Turkish domination. The Greek Orthodox Church did what it could to keep Greek religion and learning alive among the people. Finally, on 25 March 1821, *the Greek War of Independence* began when the banner of revolution was raised at the *Monastery of Kalavrita* in the Peloponnese. A long and

*14. The valley of Sparta as seen from Mistras. The town of Sparta can be seen in the background.*

bloody war followed, with Egypt aiding the Turks, and the French, English (among them Lord Byron) and Russians aiding the Greeks. Hostilities ended in 1830, when the Cyclades, Attica, and the Peloponnese won their freedom; it would take until after World War I for almost all of Greece to be free of Turkish rule.

After a brief interlude as a Republic, with its capital at Nauplion in the Peloponnese, Greece became a monarchy, with Otho of Bavaria, a German princelet (chosen by the Great Powers) as king. Otho was soon deposed, and a new king, George, imported from Denmark; a constitution severely limited the powers of the monarchy. Reclaiming the rest of Greece from the Turkish yoke dominated politics in the years to come, along with the global conflicts of the two world wars. The German occupation was particularly severe in the Peloponnese, and many roadside monuments and shrines mark where civilians were executed. Others record deaths which occurred during the bloody civil war which followed the end of World War II. Today, Greece is a Republic, having ousted the 7-year junta of "The Colonels" in 1973, and having voted the next year to end the monarchy. In 1980, Greece voted to join the EEC (Common Market), and is now a full member; hopes are, if not high, strong in the Peloponnese that EEC membership will make it possible to export Greek goods to a wider market.

## Myths and Legends

Throughout much of antiquity, the Greeks interpreted their past with *myths* and *legends*. In the long millennia before the written word made it possible to write down what had happened, there was a strong oral tradition preserving memories of what had happened. The great poet Homer was part of this tradition: Homer probably lived in the 9th century B.C., and brought together into two coherent works, the Iliad and the Odyssey, centuries worth of stories which had been sung and recited about the Trojan Wars. And, sometime later, perhaps by the great 6th-century Athenian leader *Peisistratos*, the two poems were finally written down. Although the historian

*Herodotus* (often called "the father of history") was quite critical of Homer's accuracy in dealing with the events of the Trojan War, research in the last two centuries has authenticated an astonishing amount of what Homer had to say about events he learned of from the long oral tradition. In turn, this has made scholars more open to the idea that some legends – such as the return of the Sons of Herakles – preserve kernels of truth – such as memories of the Dorian invasion. Some other myths and legends remain mysterious to us, but shaped what the ancient Greeks of the Peloponnese thought about their heritage. Here are just a few of the better-known ancient myths and legends from the Peloponnese.

Not surprisingly, many of the myths connected with the Peloponnese go back to the legendary hero Pelops from whom the peninsula takes its name. *Pelops* was the son of *Tantalus*, King of Phrygia, himself a son of *Zeus*. For reasons best known to himself, Tantalus attempted to deceive Zeus into eating Pelops, served up roasted at a banquet of the Olympian Gods. Zeus was not deceived, restored Pelops to life, and condemned

*15. A 6th-century B.C. painted wooden tablet representing a sacrificial scene, found in the village of Pitsa in Corinthia.*

Tantalus to the eternal frustration which has given us the word *"tantalize"*. The young Pelops, restored to life and health, fell in love with the maiden *Hippodameia*, daughter of the King of *Olympia*, and won her hand in marriage – but not without deceit. Hippodameia's father had said that he would give his daughter to anyone who could defeat him in a chariot race. Of course, no one could, until Pelops bribed the royal charioteer, Myrtilus, to loosen the linchpin on the king's chariot. As the king's chariot spun out of control, Pelops won the race – and promptly flung Myrtilus into the sea to protect his secret. Pelops had won the race, and won the hand of Hippodamia, but by killing Myrtilus, he had brought down a curse on his descendants.

Since Pelops' descendants were the powerful House of *Atreus*, (taking its name from the son of Pelops and Hippodameia), the curse of Myrtilus affected a good deal of Greek history. Members of the House of Atreus included the Mycenae's king *Agamemnon*, *Aegisthus*, and the Spartan king *Menelaus.* Menelaus lost his wife, Helen, to Paris of Troy, and Agamemnon was killed in his bath by his wife Clytemnestra and Aegisthus. In part, this stemmed from the curse of Myrtilus, in part from the fact that Pelops' two sons, *Atreus* and *Thysetes*, had a disastrous quarrel as a result of which Atreus deceived his brother into eating two of his children – and Thysetes placed a curse on his brother's descendants. Clearly, this curse was also powerful, and almost no one in the House of Atreus (which included *Iphigenia, Electra,* and *Orestes*) escaped its force. The tellings and retellings of the myths and legends surrounding Pelops and his descendants gave poets including Aeschylus ample material, and scenes from the gruesome family disputes are to be seen on countless Greek vases.

A cluster of myths center on ancient Argos, not far from Agamemnon's Mycenae. This was the home of Perseus, who slew the Gorgon, and it was in the Argolid that his great-grandson *Herakles* performed his labors. Although Pelops gave his name to the Peloponnese, its most beloved hero throughout antiquity was not Pelops, but Herakles. *Herakles* was the son of a mortal maiden and Zeus, and, as always, Zeus's wife Hera was not amused by the royal bastard. Hera slipped two ser-

16. *A scene on a 6th-century B.C. vase depicting one of the twelve labours of Herakles.*
17. *Another scene on an archaic vase depicting the slaying of Aegisthus by Orestes.*

18. *The village of Tyros.*
19. *A quiet beach near the village of Tyros.*

*20. An old bridge over a small river at Giannos village, Arcadia.*
*21. The monastery of Loukous in Arcadia.*

pents into Herakles's crib, but the infant woke, and strangled them – a sign of his future strength. As a youth, Herakles was driven mad by Hera, and slew several of his own children. To expiate his sin, he undertook his famous twelve labors. In rapid succession, Herakles slew the *Nemean lion*; the ferocious water monster, the *Hydra*; the fierce *Erymanthean boar*; captured a *golden stag*; destroyed the evil *Stymphalian birds*; cleaned the *Augean stables*; stole the *Cretan bull*; captured the *flesh-eating horses of Diomedes*; stole a *golden girdle from the Queen of the Amazons*; captured oxen belonging to the monster *Geryon*; stole the *golden apples of the Hesperides*, and, finally, fetched the monstrous *Cerberus* from *Hades*. Small wonder that Herakles became *the* favorite hero throughout the Peloponnese forever after! Although some of Herakles' labors seem frivolous, others (such as slaying the monsters that were making life difficult for people) clearly suggest that the burly Herakles was seen as a great benefactor of humanity, and a civilizing force in a frightening world. Indeed, to this day, Herakles' portrait adorns the bags of cement made in the Peloponnese, to suggest that today's cement is as strong as the Peloponnese's legendary hero.

# Around the Peloponnese:

## The Major Sites, the Towns and the Countryside

Those lucky enough to have the time to visit the Peloponnese at a leisurely, rather than a break-neck pace, will probably find that some of their happiest memories come from evenings spent in seaside cafes, walks in the mountain ranges, and improbable encounters with flocks of goats on dusty country lanes. However, almost all visitors will head for the major sites, and most will begin with Corinthia and the Argolid.

# Corinthia

Until 1893, ships sailing from the west to the port of Athens, Piraeus, had to make a long and difficult journey around the Peloponnese. The completion of the Corinth canal (attempted repeatedly in antiquity, most notably by the Roman emperor *Nero*) put an end to all that, and today one of the pleasures of crossing into the Peloponnese is standing above the canal and watching ships pass through. A string of fast-

*22. The isthmus of Corinth completed in 1893, separates the Peloponnese from mainland Greece.*

*23. The site of the theatre in ancient Corinth.*
*24. The Julian Basilica with the Circular Pedestal in the forefront.*
*25. Partial view of the fortification of Acrocorinth.*

food souvlakia places and souvenir shops lines the Peloponnesian side of the canal, tour buses pause here for a photo, and local buses from Athens to the Peloponnese usually make a stop at the canal to see if there are any passengers heading their way. Above the canal looms Acrocorinth, the imposing akropolis of ancient Corinth, with its extensive Venetian, Frankish, and Turkish fortifications. For centuries, whoever held Acrocorinth held the Peloponnese, and it is somewhat startling to learn that in antiquity Acrocorinth was best known for its *Temple of Aphrodite*, the home of more than 1000 temple prostitutes. One wonders if the grueling climb up Acrocorinth discouraged visitors to the Temple. From the summit there are fine views across the Gulf to the spa of *Loutraki* and the promontory with the tiny classical site of *Perachora*. In summer, the plain beneath Corinth is covered with the vineyards which produce the area's fine wines, and the cur-

*26. View of the ruins of the Agora. In the middle are seven of the surviving Doric columns from the peristyle of the Temple of Apollo.*

rants which are exported throughout the world.

Corinth had two great periods of prosperity in antiquity: the first during the 7th century B.C. when its far-flung maritime empire exported Corinthian goods (including the distinctive pottery which may be seen in the Corinth museum) across the Aegean. Some say that it was at Corinth that the distinctive longboat of antiquity, the trireme, was developed. (And, of course, the elaborate Corinthian capital was developed here). One of Corinth's tyrants, Periander, was so shrewd that he was thought to be one of the Seven Sages of Antiquity. *Periander* was the first to attempt a passing across the isthmus: not a canal, but a roadway across which ships could be pulled. At the same time, *Periander* began several of the important monuments which may be seen today at ancient Corinth: the fountain of Peirene and the Temple of Apollo.

*27. The Lechaion Road at the site of the Agora of ancient Corinth. The remains of the Julian Basilica can be seen on the right.*

*28, 29. Two different views of the interior of the Fountain of Peirene.*
*30. Six arched entrances to the Fountain of Peirene.*

*31. A large pithos, which probably belonged to an oil merchant.*
*32. Part of the Agora with the north-west shops in the background.*

*33. Remains of ancient shops found in the Agora of Corinth.*
*34. The Glauke Fountain on the west side of the Agora.*

*35. The remaining modified Corinthian columns of the peripteral Temple of Octavia, built on a podium.*
*36. A close view of the seven remaining columns of the Temple of Apollo.*
*37. Remains on the south side of ancient Corinth.*
*38. A close-up view of the Julian Basilica.*

39. The paved Lechaion road in front of the Propylaia of the Agora. Acrocorinth can be seen in the background.

Corinth's second period of prosperity came centuries later, under the Romans, who first levelled much of the city and then lavishly rebuilt it with baths, aqueducts, roads, and shrines. Consequently, almost all of the classical agora (marketplace) now lies under the extensive Roman agora. Similarly, the Greek temple was rebuilt by the Romans, who also added an Odeon (concert hall) which seated 3000. Corinth was an important site during the early Christian era as well, and *Saint Paul* himself founded a basilica at *Cenchreai*, one of Corinth's two ports. Another enormous Christian church was built at Corinth's other port, *Lechaion*. Long walls once connected both ports with Corinth, but much of the walls, and of the ancient port towns, is now beneath the sea.

Today ancient Corinth is primarily a Roman town, although the monumental *Temple of Apollo*, several stoas, a stadium, and parts of the original Fountain of Peirene remain from the classical period. The Temple of Apollo (ca. 550 B.C.) is one of the finest surviving temples in all Greece: seven of the original 38 monolithic limestone columns remain in place, and four more lie on their sides, toppled in one of the earthquakes that so frequently trouble the Peloponnese. Gone is the monumental statue of Apollo which once stood inside the temple, but even in ruins the temple is splendid, and dwarfs six nearby smaller Roman temples, such as the Temple of Octavia near the museum.

Both is classical antiquity and under the Romans, Corinth was an important commercial center, crowded with stoas, shops, and markets along broad avenues. Most would have entered Corinth through its monumental gateway at the head of the *Lechaion Road*, which ran from Corinth to the port of Lechaion. The gateway was crowned with a monumental statue of Apollo's foolish son *Phaethon*, who attempted to drive his father's chariot of the sun – and lost control of the horses and plunged to his death. Visitors on summer days, when tour groups crowd the site, should remember that Corinth would have been even more crowded in antiquity. There would have

*40. The interior of the museum of Corinth.*
*41. Headless statues outside the museum.*

42. A 7th-century B.C. early Corinthian alabaster vase with animal representations. An owl is in the centre.
43. A 7th-century B.C. Corinthian aryballos.

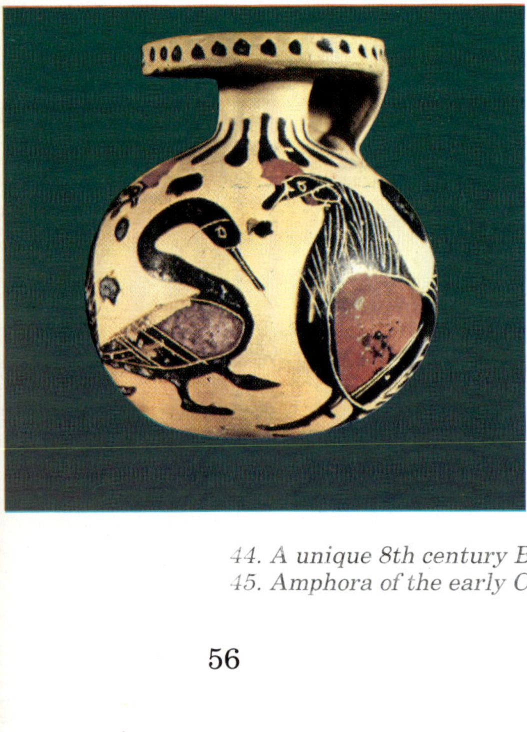

44. A unique 8th century B.C. Corinthian example of the potter's art.
45. Amphora of the early Corinthian period.

*46. A shepherd playing the flute.*
*47. Mosaic from a Roman villa with the head of Dionysos in the middle.*
*48. Gigantomachy: a relief plaque from the Roman period.*

*49.Female head of Tyche (Goddess of fortune).*

*50.Roman head of Dionysos.*

been merchants and sailors, farmers in from their fields, foreigners from all around the Aegean, and tourists drawn by the splendors of the city. In fact, in part thanks to the Temple of Aphrodite on Acrocorinth, Corinth had quite a racy reputation in antiquity, and a popular aphorism was "See Corinth and Die" – suggesting that anything after Corinth would be an anticlimax.

In Roman times, Corinth was an important administrative center, and issues of particular public importance were debated from a raised platform in the center of town known as the *bema*. Probably a considerable crowd gathered on the day in 52 A.D. when the Roman consul *Gallio* heard accusations

*51. The outer gate leading up to Acrocorinth. In front of the gate there was once a dry moat spanned by a bridge.*
*52-55. Four gates leading to Acrocorinth.*

*56. Ruins of buildings and fortifications at Cenchreai.*
*57. Remains of an ancient temple at Cenchreai.*

from Corinth's Jewish community that *Saint Paul* was a heretic, and troublemaker. After listening to testimony from the *bema* (almost completely restored), Gallio dismissed all the charges against Saint Paul. Records of the hearing were probably stored in the *Tabularium*, or *civic archives*, once flanked by a long terrace ornamented with more than 100 statues of emperors and governors. Nearby was the southern portico, with a long row of shops, many of which were taverns, where weary visitors could rest in the shade, and drink wine, or water piped in from the nearby *Peirene* spring. Today's visitors must make do with the little cafes outside the excavations, or get a drink of cool water in the pleasant museum courtyard.

*58. The three remaining columns of the Temple of Zeus at Nemea.*

*59. The village of ancient Corinth.*
*60. Part of the Isthmian walls.*

*61. Loutra (baths) Tis Oraias Elenis (Helen of Troy).*
*62. Korfos village.*

*63, 64. The resort town of Loutraki, across the Gulf of Corinth.*

Corinth was not only a thriving commercial center, but the center of one of the great events of antiquity: the Isthmian games. These took place every two years from 582 B.C. near the sanctuary of Poseidon on the isthmus, and careful excavations have restored the stadium and even some of the racetracks and starting gates. The Roman emperor Nero competed in the Isthmian games; not surprisingly, he won his events.

Corinth overshadows Corinthia today, as it did in antiquity, although a cluster of nearby ancient sites such as *Sicyon, Cleonae,* and *Nemea* have their charms. Nemea, like Isthmia, was the site of *pan-Hellenic* games, perhaps founded to commemorate Herakles' slaying of the fierce Nemean lion. The recently restored 4th-century temple of Nemea and a pleasant small museum (as well as an excellent local wine, known as "Herakles's blood") make this a pleasant spot to stop on the way from Corinth into the Argolid.

65, 66. Two views of Vouliagmeni beach near Perachora.

*67. The Roman aqueduct a few metres away from the Temple of Athena at Lourtaki.*
*68, 69. The Heraion at Perachora. The foundations of the Temple of Hera Akraia and the altar can be seen.*

## Argolid

Corinthia and the Argolid have rich fields of olives, vineyards, and grain, and gentle hills and mountains, although the pass from Corinthia into the Argolid is a narrow, somewhat mysterious, winding gorge known as the *Dervenakia Pass*. The road, lovely when not crowded, can be something of an endurance contest in summer, when tour buses and farm vehicles contend to take up the maximum amount of road space. While Corinthia is dominated by Corinth itself, the Argolid has a cluster of important ancient sites: Mycenae, Epidauros, Argos – and one of the loveliest towns in Greece, Nauplion, on the Argo-Saronic Gulf. From seaside towns such as Porto Kheli, there are fine views out toward the islands of Hydra and Spetses, which can easily be visited by taking the Flying Dolphin hydrofoil from Porto Kheli itself.

Mycenae straddles a low hill between two conical mountains, and dominates the plain outside Argos. Today, the little modern village of Mycenae lies just off the Corinth-Argos road, just below the ancient site itself. A string of hotels, restaurants, and souvenir stands announce that one is nearing Mycenae, but the site itself always comes as something of a surprise: rearing up out of the plain, mysterious, despite all the tour buses parked at its base. This is the home of the ill-starred *House of Atreus*, and it is difficult not to remember Agamemnon's fateful homecoming as one toils up the hill to Mycenae. Agamemnon, after returning home to Greece in triumph after winning the Trojan War, and reclaiming his brother Menelaus's wife Helen, met his death here at the hands of his wife Clytemnestra and her lover Aigestheus. Clytemnestra acted to revenge Agamemnon's sacrifice of their daughter *Iphigenia*, and *Aegisthus* acted to revenge Agamemnon's father's deception of *his* father. Agamemnon's son *Orestes* then slew his mother and Aegisthus to avenge his father's death, and was forever after pursued by the Furies. In addition, Agamemnon and Clytemnestra's one remaining child, Electra, was driven mad. Mycenae, in short, is one of history's fateful places, more bloody than the Bloody Tower of London!

*70. The impressive triangular stone relief over the Lion Gate at Mycenae.*
*71. The Lion Gate as seen from inside the citadel.*
*72. The Lion Gate (frontal view).*

*73, 74. Two views of the Acropolis of Mycenae showing the Cyclopean walls. The palace is on the summit.*

*75, 76. Masses of tourists arrive in hordes each year to view the fascinating remains of the Acropolis at Mycenae.*

77. The Tholos tomb known as the "Tomb of Clytemnestra".
78. The "Tomb of Agamemnon" also known as the "Treasury of Atreus".
79. The inside of the "Treasury of Atreus".

It is clear that Mycenae was a superb fortress: it is encircled by defensive walls, and sealed by the magnificent *Lion Gate*. Mycenae had its own water supply, from a cistern deep in the earth, still visible beneath a slippery flight of stairs. The palace sprawls across the hill, with a rabbit warren of small rooms, but two rooms – the *throne room* and the *great hall* (*megaron*) are quite distinct. These are the state chambers where Agamemnon and the other kings of Mycenae would have received visitors, and conducted business. Perhaps it was in one of these rooms that Menelaus told his brother Agamemnon of Helen's infidelity, and convinced Agamemnon to lead the expedition to Troy to fetch her home. Certainly it was in one of these rooms that Agamemnon met his death, and it was in one of the shaft graves just inside the Lion Gate that he was buried. The golden tomb treasures of Mycenae, including the *"Mask of Agamemnon"*, were found in 1874 by the great archaeologist *Schliemann* in the shaft graves (dated to the *Early Mycenaean period*, 1580-1500 B.C.). The majestic beehive (*tholos*) tombs just outside the citadel date from the Middle Mycenaean period (1500-1425 B.C.), and yet other tholos tombs, along with the defense walls, date from the Late Mycenaean period (1425-1100 B.C.).

Mycenae's defense walls indicate that it was endangered; until the Late Mycenaean period, there had been no need for such walls. Scholars still debate what led to the fall of Mycenae, and whether, in fact, the "Mask of Agamemnon" could have been Agamemnon's. Perhaps one should remember the words of the English philhellene *Robert Liddell* who once wrote that, "Mycenae is one of the most ancient and fabulous places in Europe. I think it should be visited first for the fable, next for the lovely landscape, and thirdly for the excavations...".

Although Mycenae dominated the plain of Argos, it was not the only important site of its time: just outside Nauplion is *Tiryns*, which Homer described as "well-walled". The walls are as much as 25 feet thick, and once rose to more than twice their present height. Presumably, Tiryns was a dependency of Mycenae, and, like Mycenae, it seems to have been virtually destroyed around 1200 B.C. From Tiryns, the Venetian forti-

*80. The foundations of several houses, probably residences of wealthy merchants (13th-century B.C.).*
*81. Grave Circle A*

33

fications on the peaks above Argos, as well as the massive fortifications above Nauplion are clearly visible, reminding visitors of the powers which came after the Mycenaean empire.

Argos was so important in early antiquity that Homer sometimes uses *"the Argives"* to mean "the Greeks". Still, as long as Mycenae flourished, Argos was checked, and Argos's main period of prosperity came in the 7th century B.C. under

*82. The so-called gold "Mask of Agamemnon" dating from the Early Mycenean period, 1500-1425 B.C.*
*83. Fresco found southwest of the Cult centre depicting a Mycenean lady.*

*84. The main entrance of the Acropolis of Tiryns, leading to the Palace.*
*85. One of the galleries at the Acropolis of Tiryns.*
*86. The site of ancient Tiryns.*

*87. The inside of one of the galleries at Tiryns.*

88.A Gold ring (the largest ever found) depicting a religious scene.
89. A fresco depicting a boar being hunted by three dogs.

the legendary king *Pheidon*. Nothing remains of this Argos, and during the next century, Corinth rather overshadowed Argos. Still, during the 5th-century B.C., this was the home of several famous sculptors, notably *Polykleitos*. Excavations have revealed parts of the 5th-century B.C. agora, where the head of Medusa was thought to have been buried by the hero Perseus. Nearby there is a large 4th-century B.C. theater, Roman baths and an Odeon. Finds from the excavations, including some Roman mosaics, are on display in the small museum in the center of town. Just outside town are the impressive remains of the Argive Heraion, the ancient town's main shrine. Today modern Argos has little charm, as repeated earthquakes have levelled its older buildings. Yet during the 7th century B.C., this was one of the most important towns in the Pelopon-

*90. The city of Argos as seen from the fort of Larissa, overlooking the city.*

*92. The theatre of Argos, one of the largest in antiquity.*
*93. The Roman Odeon at Argos.*

*91. A general view of the theatre and the surrounding area.*
*94. The remains of the 2nd century B.C. Roman baths.*

95, 96. *Two views of the church of "Zoodochos Pigi" at Kephalari near Argos.*

nese, thanks in part to the fertile farmland which still surrounds it.

If Argos is one of the least charming towns in the Peloponnese, *Nauplion* is surely one of the most lovely. Nauplion straddles a small peninsula, jutting into the Argolic Gulf, with views of the mountain ranges of the Peloponnese. During the Middle Ages, Greeks, Franks, and Venetians occupied Nauplion, and built the massive fortifications on the acropolis above the town. After independence, Nauplion was briefly Greece's capital, and, as a result, it has a number of delightful neo-classical buildings (as well as one or two forlorn mosques). A road runs above Nauplion to the *Palamidi* and *Acronauplia* fortifications, and there are splendid views across the bay from the ramparts. In the harbour is the miniature kastro the *Bourtzi*, a great favorite of photographers in search of a scenic shot who perhaps do not know that the Bourtzi was once a home for retired executioners. Nauplion has a delightful quay with cafes, a lovely square with a crumbling mosque, and two fine museums, one of antiquities, and one the headquarters of the Peloponnesian Folklore Society. There are excellent beaches nearby at *Tolo* and *Porto Kheli*, and excursions to the small neolithic site of Lerna, as well as the major site of Epi-

*97. Nauplion: A view of the fortified islet of Bourtzi.*

98. The fortified hill of Acronauplia, the town of Nauplion and Bourtzi, as seen from th
99. Another view of Bourtzi. Nea Kios and Miloi are in the background.

*lamidi fortress.*

*100. The "Rock" of Palamidi.*

*101. An old Turkish Mosque as it stands today.*

*102, 103. Typical streets in the town of Nauplion.*
*104. A spectacular view of the town of Nauplion at dusk.*

105. Following pages: *A panoramic view of Acronauplia, Nauplion and one of its beaches.*

*106. The fortress of Palamidi which looms over the Argolid.*
*107-111. Different views of the fortress of Palamidi.*

*112. The picturesque village of Methana.*
*113. The village of Porto-Kheli.*

*114, 115. The village of Tolo with two of its beaches.*

dauros, make Nauplion a delightful spot to stay.

*Epidauros* was the shrine of the healing god, *Aesclepios*, and an important pilgrimage spot. Foundations of the ancient healing shrines, temples, and dormitories where visitors stayed are scattered through a lovely pine grove. The excavation museum has any number of thanks-inscriptions and votive offerings left by pilgrims to the sanctuary. But most come to Epidauros today to see its theater, which seats 14,000, and is used in July and August for a drama festival. Performances begin as the sun sinks over the hills behind the stage, and if one has visited Mycenae that morning, and the play is the "Agamemnon", the tragic history of the House of Atreus seems very close indeed.

*116. Ruins of buildings on the site of Palia Epidauros.*

117, 118. *Part of the remains of Epidauros, the cradle of ancient Greek theatre.*

*119. The ruins of the Roman Odeon of Epidauros.*
*120. Part of the Katagogeion.*
*121. The ruins of the Gymnasium of ancient Epidauros.*

*122, 123. Two views of the Tholos, the most ornate and elaborate structure in Epidauros.*

*124, 125. The best preserved theatre in Greece, the theatre of Epidauros, is a marvel of grace and proportion, fulfilling every architect's dream of perfect aestheticism.*

*126. Detail from the sanctuary of Asklepios found in the Epidauros museum.*

*127. The Corinthian column and part of the ceiling of the Tholos, one of the most beautiful exhibits in the museum of Epidauros.*

*128. The marble statue of the goddess Athena in the museum of Epidauros.*
*129. The statue of the goddess Hygeia (Health) in the same museum.*

130, 131. *Two Ionic columns and other decorative pieces in front of the museum of Epidauros.*

*132-134. The remains of the 4th-century B.C. stadium of Epidauros.*

*135. An islet situated opposite the seaside village of Tolo.*

*136, 137. Two views of the village of Palia Epidauros.*

*138. Sunset at Palia Epidauros.*
*139. The small theatre of Palia Epidauros.*

# Arcadia

From the Argolid, many visitors head towards Sparta in Laconia, and on the way they pass through part of *Arcadia*, on the road from Argos to Sparta via Tripoli, Arcadia's capital. Tripoli is an energetic town of no particular architectural distinction, and it is a pity that more visitors do not deviate from the fastest route to Sparta, and do not spent a bit of time exploring Arcadia itself. The mountain villages of Arcadia have some of the nicest architecture (and some of the finest monasteries and convents, such as Eleonas, near Kosmas) in the Peloponnese, and seaside towns like *Aghios Andreas* and *Astros* offer good beaches beneath the mighty Parnon mountain range. In addition, parts of Arcadia are as well-watered now as they were in antiquity, when Arcadia was almost

*140. A general view of the ancient site of Tegea.*

symonymous with the ideal countryside for poets from *Theocritus* to *Ovid*.

Three of the most impressive ancient sites in Arcadia are near Tripoli: *Mantineia, Tegea,* and *Megalopolis*, and two – Mantineia and Megalopolis – have associations with the great *Theban* leader *Epaminondas*, who "liberated" Arcadia from the Spartans in the 4th century B.C. Epaminondas founded Megalopolis (the name simply means "great town") to be the new center of Arcadia, and gave it an enormous theater which could seat 21,000, and an impressive array of governmental buildings. Soon after Megalopolis was begun, Epaminondas died in battle at Mantineia, and the town withered away. The

*141. The remains of the Temple of Athena Alea at Tegea.*
*142. The magnificent monastery of Panaya Elona.*

143. *The monastery of St John the Baptist.*
144. *A monument commemorating those fallen in battle, built with materials from the ancient site at Mantineia.*
145. *The church of Agia Photini at Mantineia, built partly with material taken from the ancient site.*

*146. The ancient theatre at Mantineia.*
*147. The theatre of Megalopolis, the largest in antiquity.*
*148. The tiny church of Agia Theodora, near the village of Issari. Over a dozen trees grow on its roof.*
*149.* Following Pages: *The picturesque village of Astros in eastern Arcadia.*

extensive ramparts of Mantineia, where Epaminondas died, trying to look out toward Megalopolis, are still in place. As for Tegea, although it was an important town in antiquity, and the home of the great temple of *Athena Alea*, decorated by the great 4th century sculptor *Skopas*, it was also an important town centuries later under the Franks. There are remains of walls, and several churches to remind visitors of the days when French speaking knights ruled Arcadia.

150, 151. *The monastery of the Transfiguration of the Saviour Loukous.*

*152. The village of Karitena, seen from the castle.*
*153. The historic village of Dimitsana.*

*154. A hotel and other houses in Stemnitsa.*
*155. A view of the village of Stemnitsa.*

*156. Astros beach: one of the most beautiful in the Peloponnese.*
*157. The town of Leonidion in eastern Arcadia.*

*158, 159. Two views of the picturesque village of Issari halfway between the ancient site of Licossoura and the Church of Agia Theodora.*

# Laconia

In antiquity, *Laconia* – and much of the Peloponnese – was dominated by Sparta; while the rest of Greece experimented with different forms of government, exchanging kings for tyrants, tyrants for oligarchies, and oligarchies for democracies, *Sparta* main-

*160. The majestic hill of Mistras as seen from its base.*

tained a conservative form of government throughout its history. The Spartan economy rested on the shoulders of the helots, the class of slaves who did all the agricultural work, leaving the Spartans free to concentrate on defense and conquest. Spartan youths left home at 7 and lived in dormitories, where they were trained for future military service. Spartan girls had an unusual amount of freedom, and other Greeks

*161, 162. Running spring water at the verdant village of Tripi on the slopes of Mt. Taïyetos.*
*163. A road running through one of the numerous gorges of Mt. Taïyetos, connecting Sparta with Kalamata.*

were shocked by their independence. Sparta produced many great generals, but no artists and writers; it was a harsh society, and has given us the word "laconic" from "Laconian".

Sparta's superb natural position, encircled by the Taïyetos and *Parnon* ranges, led to its isolation from the rest of Greece. Still, when the Persians invaded in 490 B.C. and again in 480 B.C., Sparta sent a contingent (under the famous general *Leonidas*) to fight with the other Greeks against Persia. During much of the 5th century, Athens and Sparta fought the Peloponnesian War (431-404 B.C.); when it was over, Sparta had won, but exhausted itself in the process. Thereafter, Sparta's glory lay behind it. In later centuries, Franks, Venetians, and Byzantines contended for control of the area, founding important fortresses and cities at *Geraki, Monemvassia,* and *Mistras.*

*164. The museum of Sparta.*

Today Sparta is a pleasant town with wide avenues, spectacularly situated at the foot of the Taïyetos range. In antiquity, the Spartans boasted that they had no need for defense walls, thanks to the encircling mountain ranges of Taïyetos and Parnon. The remains of ancient Sparta are meager, and remind one of the great historian *Thucydides's* prediction that no one in the future would ever believe that Sparta had been one of the two great powers in Greece. Sparta's agora has not yet been excavated, and its once great theater was almost entirely carted off centuries ago, stone by stone, to build Mistras. From where the theater was, one has a spectacular view of the

*165. A magnificent view of Mistras.*

rich plain of Sparta, cut through by the mighty *Eurotas River*, towards Taïyetos and *Mistras*.

Mistras straddles a conical hill, and commands a superb view of the plain. The town was first settled in the 9th century A.D. by refugees fleeing the Slavic invasions of the Peloponnese, but its greatest prominence came when it was the Byzantine capital of Morea (1349-1460). Nothing can prepare the visitor for Mistras, a virtual ghost town, crowned by the Palace of the Despots, and boasting streets of once-fine houses and elegantly decorated churches. It was in Mistras's cathedral church that the last Byzantine emperor, Constantine XII

*166.* Following Pages: *View of Mistras; the castle crowns the summit. The church of Pantanassa and other buildings.*

Palaeologos, was crowned in 1433. A marble stone with the double-headed eagle of Byzantium marks the spot.

Mistras was by no means the only important center in Laconia during the medieval period, and nearby Geraki has a superb fortress, defense walls, and splendid churches. And one of the Peloponnese's greatest fortresses, Monemvassia, at the tip of the westernmost prong of the Peloponnese, boasts the 13th century church of Aghia Sophia along with almost 40 small Byzantine churches. Unlike the ghost town Mistras,

167. Preceding Pages: *The Byzantine church of Pantanassa in Mistras.*

*168. A breathtaking view from the castle of Monemvassia. The church of Agia Sophia is perched on the edge of the cliff.*

*169. The main square of the village of Monemvassia. The castle walls are in the background.*

170. Following Pages: *The awesome "Rock of Monemvassia" crowned by the castle. The village of Monemvassia is behind the rock.*

171. The village of Monemvassia, with its many churches and red-tiled roofs.

Monemvassia is undergoing something of a rebirth, with many of the old houses renovated by wealthy Athenians and foreigners. Monemvassia gave its name to the Malmsey wine (Malmsey is a corruption of Malvoisie, from Monemvassia) that passed through this port *en route* to European markets.

Northwest of Monemvassia is *Gythion*, the port of ancient Sparta, today a charming seaside town with a lovely harbour, lined with restaurants advertising "fresh fish, whatever you want". In the harbour is the tiny island of *Kranai*, where, legend has it, *Helen* and *Paris* spent their "honeymoon night" after they fled Sparta. From here they would have set out on the long voyage to Troy – soon to be pursued by Helen's husband Menelaus, his brother Agamemnon, and the forces of the Greek armies. Today Gythion is a jumping-off point for a visit to the tower towns of the Mani, the most isolated section of Laconia, and a tour of the famous cave of Dirou, where neolithic remains have been found. And, from Gythion, one can set forth for distant Crete and the off-shore island of *Kythera*.

*172. The ancient theatre of Gythion.*

173, 174. *The town of Gythion as seen from the tiny island of Kranai.*

175, 176. *The villages of Limeni and Neo Oitilo on the northwestern side of the Mani peninsula.*
177. *The church and the bell-tower of Agii Taxiarkhes at Areopoli.*

ΔΩΜΑΤΙΑ
ROOMS

*178. The pebble beach of Gherolimenas on the southwest coast of the Mani peninsula.*
*180. The majestic towers in the village of Vatheia on the tip of the Mani peninsula.*

*179. View of the tiny church of Panayia Vlacherna and the adjoining tower at Mezapos.*

181. Typical Byzantine church at Gheraki, Laconia.
182. The church of Agii Taxiarkhes at Charouda.

*183, 184. Two of the numerous little churches found throughout Mani: St. Petros (12th century) and St. Georgios and Aikaterini at Dryalos.*
*185. A panoramic view of the bay of Limeni.*

*186. A view of the fantastic Dirou Cave.*

# Kythera

Although *Kythera* is just off the coast of the Peloponnese it (like Hydra, Spetses, and Poros) is administered from distant Piraeus. Like many of the islands of the Ionian and Aegean, Kythera has been affected by mass emigration, and there are many more Kytherans today in Australia than on the island itself. In antiquity, Kythera was famous for production of a highly valued purple dye made from the shell of the murex. The rich murex beds drew *Minoan* and *Phoenician* settlers to Kythera, and there are a few Minoan remains at *Kastri*, as well as classical remains at *Paliokastro*. In addition, many believe that the church of Aghios Kosmas stands on the site of the ancient shrine to *Aphrodite*, who was believed to have been born at Kythera. Yet Kythera's main attractions are its pleasant beaches and towns such as *Chora*, with its extensive Venetian remains. The beauty of the island is such that one can easily understand why the ancients believed that this was the birthplace of Aphrodite.

*187. A view of Kapsali.*

188. *General view of Kythera or Chora and Kapsali village.*
189, 190. *Cannons and a little church overlooking the harbour.*
191. *A closer view of the shore. The monastery of St. Demetrios is in the background.*
192. *The monastery of St. Demetrios near Kapsali, set amongst craggy cliffs.*

193. *The castle overlooking Chora.*
194. *The castle and part view of Chora.*

# Messenia

*Messenia* has always been one of the richest areas in the Peloponnese: the Spartans fought a series of wars to conquer and add it to their own territory. After the decline of Sparta, Epaminondas seized Messenia, and established the new town of *Messene*. Under the Roman occupation, Messenia was something of a backwater, but during the Middle Ages, Franks and Venetians contended for control of this fertile area. As a result, Messenia has some of the finest castles in the Pelopon-

*195. The well-preserved theatre of Messene.*
*196. Petalidi beach between Kalamata and Koroni.*
*197. Part of the walls of the castle of Navarino (Neokastro). The island of Sphacteria is in the background.*

*198. The picturesque town of Pylos.*
*199. A panoramic view of Kalamata and its long pebbly beach. The village of Almyros is in the foreground.*
*200. Methoni: The Bourtzi as it appears through one of the gates of the castle.*

nese, at *Navarino, Methoni, Koroni,* and at *Kalamata*, Messenia's otherwise undistinguished capital city.

*Methoni* and *Koroni* guard the eastern and western approaches to Messenia, and were of enormous strategic importance, not merely during the Middle Ages, but centuries later during the Greek War of Independence. Methone has a long history: Homer tells us that Agamemnon offered Achilles the fortress of Methoni in exchange for Achilles's slave woman *Brisies* whom Agamemnon coveted. During the middle ages. Methoni was an important stopping off point for pilgrims *en route* to the Holy Land, and the entire area was important in the silk trade. Today, the fortress at Methoni is one of the most impressive sights in the Peloponnese, with its moats, fortifications, and the remnants of the barracks and chapels which served the soldiers stationed here. Koroni, although magnificent, suffers by comparison with Methoni, which was always larger, and is better preserved. The Castle of Arcadia at Kiparissia on the western coast of Messenia is also splendid, and the town of Kiparissia has all the charm that Kalamata lacks.

*201. Methoni: A view of the castle and the aqueduct.*

*202. A castle gateway. A Bembo column stands on the right.*
*203. The castle of Methoni. The bridge on the left connects the castle to the Bourtzi.*

204. *Partial view of the fort of Koroni.*
205. *Byzantine churches inside the fort of Koroni.*

206. The town of Koroni with the fort in the background.
207. The town of Koroni, the port and the jetty.

208. *Methoni beach.*
209. *A view of the castle of Methoni from the east.*

210, 211. Different views of the Agora of ancient Messene.
212, 213. Part of the fortification wall of Messene.

The fortresses of Messenia were not only important during the Middle Ages, but long after, when Greeks and Turks contended fiercely for their control. One of the most critical battles of the war – the battle of Navarino in 1827 – took place in the Bay of Navarino beneath the Venetian fortress which crowns the hill above the modern village of *Pylos*. With its impressive harbour and castles, Pylos is one of the loveliest towns in the Peloponnese, and the perfect place to stay while

*214. The Byzantine church of Aghios Spyridon at Kardamyli.*
*215. A Byzantine church at Neokastro, Pylos.*
*216. Partial view of the town of Pylos.*

visiting one of the most romantic sites in the Peloponnese: the *Palace of King Nestor* at sandy Pylos.

*Nestor*, of course, was the wise old king of Pylos who always had more than a word of advice for Agamemnon and the other Greeks at Troy. Nestor's palace at what Homer called "sandy Pylos" was excavated in the 1930s, and, astonishingly, the first day's excavations unearthed the first Linear B tablets found on mainland Greece. Linear B was the script used by the Minoans and Myceneans for record keeping; in 1952, the script was deciphered by Michael Ventris, who demonstrated that it was essentially Greek. This was an important discovery, for it established that the lineage of the Greek language was even older than suspected.

There is something magical about Pylos, despite the presence of a hideous plastic roof over the excavations. The palace sits on a low hill, with views out to the sea, and farm fields beneath. There are pine trees and breezes, and, unlike *Mycenae* and *Tiryns*, which seem to bake malevolently in the sun, *Pylos* usually seems cool and pleasant. Like Mycenae and Tiryns, Pylos seems to have been destroyed ca. 1200 B.C.; throughout the palace there are scorch marks on the stone and plaster, and charred beams suggest a major conflagration. Traces remain of the lively decorative frescoes which would have adorned both stories of the original palace.

The throne room (or *megaron*) at Pylos, with its enormous circular ceremonial altar, dominates the palace. Perhaps it was in this room that Nestor received Odysseus's son *Telemachos*, and, doubtless, gave him some advice on how to find his wandering father. The royal apartments at Pylos are especially well-preserved as compared to Mycenae and Tiryns, and there is a perfectly preserved royal bathtub in place by the king's bedroom. It is nice to imagine that this may have been the tub in which Nestor's young daughter bathed Telemachos, after his long journey from Sparta to Pylos.

*217. A 15th-century B.C. chamber tomb near the Palace of Nestor.*

*218. Reconstruction of the upper floor of the Palace of Nestor.*
*219. Reconstruction of the presence chamber. In the centre a great ceremonial hearth can be seen.*

220. *A ceremonial hearth in the Palace of Nestor.*
221. *View of the bathroom with its fixed terracotta tub (larnax) still in place.*
222. *Staircase leading to the upper floor.*

*223. Mycenean gold cups from the tombs of Peristeria.*
*224. A pithos (large earthenware storage jar), found in the palace, is now outside the museum.*
*225. Another pithos used to store oil or water.*

*226. A little island off the coast of Kardamyli.*
*227. A view of the coast of Kardamyli.*

*228. The castle of Kyparissia overlooking the town.*
*229. The town of Zakharo, between the sea and the lagoon of Kaïaphas, in Elis.*

*230. A little church in the middle of vineyards in southern Messenia.*
*231. The lagoon of Kaïaphas. The water comes from springs in two large sulphurous caverns.*

# Elis

*Elis* was famous in antiquity as the home of *Olympia*, perhaps the most famous site in the Peloponnese; today the ancient site lies just outside the modern village of Olympia, which is crowded with hotels, restaurants, and tourist shops. Olympia's splendid new museum is one of the finest in the Peloponnese, with superb displays of temple sculpture, pottery, and bronzes.

Every four years from 776 B.C. to 393 A.D. athletes from all over the Greek world came to Olympia to participate in the games. During the late summer months when the games took place, a truce was observed throughout the Greek world, and all armed hostilities ceased. Like Messenia, Elis has several strong rivers, and two, the *Alpheios* and the *Peneios*, figure in numerous Greek myths: it was, for example, the Alpheios that Herakles used to clean the Augean Stables.

It was at Olympia that Pelops contended for the hand of Hippodameia, and some say that the Olympic games were founded to commemorate Pelops's victory. Others say that Herakles founded the games to commemorate completing his twelve labors. Scenes showing Pelops's chariot race decorated the east pediment of the *Temples of Zeus* at Olympia, while scenes of the *Twelve Labors of Herakles* were shown on sculptured panels on the temple.

Like the site of Corinth, Olympia is vast, and difficult for the amateur to interpret. Fortunately, unlike Corinth, Olympia is shaded with pine trees, and a delightful spot to sit and imagine the sanctuary thronged with athletes and spectators. There are really *two* Olympias, the religious sanctuary and the athletic complex. The sanctuary is dominated by the great temples of Zeus and Hera, and streets lined with buildings where the priests and administrators of Olympia lived, along with treasuries where various Greek cities stored prizes won in the athletic contests. Near the temples of Zeus and Hera is the shrine believed to mark the spot where Pelops himself was buried – a fitting resting place for the hero who gave his name to the Peloponnese.

A short walk from Pelops's tomb is the athletic complex

*232. The 4th-century B.C. stadium of Olympia.*
*233. Part of the Olympic Games ceremony.*

*234-236. Different views of the Heraion, the oldest temple in Olympia (600- B.C.).*

*237. The spring (on the right), the temple of Hera (in the middle), and the Palaistra just visible (in the background).*

*238. The remains of the once majestic Temple of Zeus.*
*239. Another view of the Heraion.*

*240. The Metroon, built in the 4th-century B.C., was dedicated to Hera, mother of the gods.*
*241-243. Three more views of the remains of the Temple of Zeus.*

which may have been built to commemorate his victory in the chariot race in which he won the hand of Hippodameia. Originally, the stadium could hold 40,000 spectators, and some say that Herakles himself paced off its length. Nearby was the Hippodrome, where chariot races were held. The games lasted five days, with contests held by day, and theatrical events by night. Women were not allowed to attend under penalty of death, however we know of one who did, and lived to tell the tale: *Pherenike*, who accompanied her fatherless son to the games. When her deceit was discovered, her life was spared in deference to her deceased husband, himself an Olympic victor, and her son, also a victor in the games.

*244, 245. Two views of the Palaistra built during the Hellenistic Period.*

*246. A section of the Gymnasium of Olympia, built in the 2nd-century B.C.*
*247, 248. The vaulted passage of "Krypte", the official entrance to the stadium, was built during the Hellenistic Period.*

*249-251. Different views of the foundations of the Leonidion, built in the mid-4th century B.C. as a guest house.*

*252, 253. Two views of an early Christian basilica built on the foundations of Pheidias' workshop.*

Inland from Olympia is one of the loveliest villages in the Peloponnese, *Andritsaina*, and one of its most impressive temples, *Bassae*. Olympia has all the hustle and bustle today that one imagines it had in antiquity when the games were in session; by contrast. Bassae is remote, isolated, and serene. The temple was built ca. 420 B.C. as a thanks offering to Apollo for warding off a fearful plague. For some years, its austere columns of local limestone have been shrouded in scaffolding preparatory to rumored restorations. Despite the scaffolding, the temple is one of the finest sights in the Peloponnese, set in lovely mountain countryside. Andritsaina itself, with overhanging balconies, slate roofs, neoclassical shop façades, and a spring with the sweetest water in all Greece, is a delight.

*254. The Philippeion, a circular structure built by Philippe of Macedon to the west of the temple of Hera.*

255. The treasury of Sikyon.

256. A view of the stone steps leading to the Metroon.

257. Another view of the Treasury of Sikyon.

258. Partial view of the podium of Herod Atticus.

*259. The statue of Nike (Victory) of Paeonios, 5th century B.C.*

*260. The statue of Nike of Paeonios today, the museum of Olympia.*

*261. The famous statue of Hermes by Praxiteles (300 B.C.), found in the Heraion, originally depicts Hermes holding a bunch of grapes in his right hand and the infant Dionysos in his left.*

262. *"Hippodameia, struggling to free herself from the Centaur Eurythion", part of a composition from the west pediment of the Temple of Zeus.*

*263. Apollo, the central figure on the west pediment of the Temple of Zeus.*

*264. The Temple of Epikourios Apollon at Bassae.*
*265. The temple is now covered as a protection from further deterioration.*

*266, 267. The remains of the Temple of Epikourios Apollon.*

*268. The village of Andritsaina, near Bassae.*
*269. The seaside village of Katakolon.*
*270. Sunset over Patra.*

## Achaia

Many visitors enter or leave Greece through the Peloponnese's largest port, Patras, in *Achaia*; this was *Byron's* first stop in Greece in 1809. The streets around the harbour are, to put it mildly, lively, with ticket agents contending for customers, dazed foreigners searching for their ship to Italy, or train to Athens, and trucks loading and unloading cargos in the middle of streets. A number of hotels along the harbor offer the possibility of a fitful night's sleep listening to the trucks, cars, and boats coming and going on the quayside. Patras is of no particular architectural interest; the Turks thoroughly destroyed the town in 1821, and it was later rebuilt around several pleasant open squares. As for Achaia itself, it takes in much of the southern shore of the Gulf of Corinth, as well as the wide Gulf of Patras. Patras itself is in a strategic position over-

*271. A general view of the city of Patra from the castle. The mountains of central Greece can be seen in the background.*

looking both its own Gulf and the Gulf of Corinth. The Roman emperor *Augustus* was just one of many who recognized Patras's strategic importance and fortified the town. Still, Patras's most impressive fortifications are the Byzantine, Frankish, Venetian and Turkish castle ruins which crown Patras's ancient acropolis. The walk to the top is not easy, but the views over the harbor are superb. Beneath the *kastro* is a *Roman odeon* where concerts are held to this day.

Achaia has no major archeological sites, but its shore has a string of lovely seaside villages, which those exhausted from too much archaeology may enjoy. South of Patras are the villages of *Kato Achaia*, and *Kalogria* and *Kounoupeli* on the *Araxos* peninsula have fine beaches. The northern shore of the Gulf of Corinth is a succession of seaside villages and resorts,

*272. The castle of Patra on top of a hill overlooking the city.*

with a scattering of new hotels at *Rion*, where one catches the ferry across to the northern shore of the Gulf of Corinth.

In addition, the area around *Kalavrita* has a number of small, delightful upland mountain villages. Kalavrita itself can be reached by a nerve-wracking narrow gauge train from *Dhiakofto*. *En route* it is possible to visit the *monastery of Mega Spilaion*, with its extensive collection of icons. Kalavrita itself is famous in modern Greek history as the site of several ferocious massacres under the Turks, and a particularly bloody massacre under the Germans. On December 15, 1943, all 1436 "men" over the age of fifteen in Kalavrita were herded into the local school house and murdered. The village was then torched.

Today, as a reminder of these events, the village clock still stands at 2.34, the time of the massacre. Such fearful events seem distant today in Kalavrita, a pleasant town with clear, cool breezes, open tavernas shaded by plane trees, and pleasant walks in the nearby country. One such walk leads to the *monastery of Aghia Lavra*, where the *Patriarch Germanos* raised the standard of revolt against the Turks on 25 March 1821 in the opening moments of the War of Independence – which, like so much else in Greek history, began in the Peloponnese.

The Peloponnese is the stuff travel posters are made of: quiet harbors, cafe tables by a harbour, sunsets over mountain ranges. It is also a world of proud and independent people – whose patience has all too often been strained to the breaking – point by foreigners who seem to think nothing of littering beaches, carousing in cafes, and ignoring local customs. Pelops's Island is a special world, even for Greece, and should be treated as just that by all who visit. Some will spend their time here exploring the major archaeological sites, while others explore the mountain ranges of Parnon and Taïyetos. Still others will head straight for a beach and move as little as possible until they have to head home. Most will try to combine a bit of serious sightseeing with a bit of relaxation – but all who come to the Peloponnese will discover that they've come to the right spot, and almost all will plan to come again as soon as possible.

*273. A large clock in the city centre decorated with flowers.*
*274. A statue of Patriarch Germanos in the central square of Patra.*

*275. The neoclassical building of the Apollo Theatre.*
*276, 277. Scenes from the famous annual Carnival of Patra.*

*278, 280. A sample of the wonderful pebbly beaches of Achaia.*

*281. The monastery of Mega Spilaion stands at the base of huge rocks.*

*282. The entrance to the monastery of Mega Spilaion.*

*283. A cavern in the interior of the monastery, where the miraculous icon of the "Mother of God" was found.*

*284, 287. The church of Panayia Trypiti stands in an attractive garden.*
*288. The tree-lined beach in front of Aigio.*

*289, 291. The Kalavrita Railway engineered in 1890. On its trip to and from Kalavrita it passes through a fantastic gorge. Examples of new and old engines.*

*292, 293. Mountainous country and grassland in Zakhlorou.*

**To our readers:**

We have made every effort to ensure that all information given here was correct at the time of publication. It is not possible, however, for any tourist guide to keep abreast of the many changes constantly being made year to year. The publishers would be pleased to be informed about any errors, omissions or complaints.